# THIS IS
# THAILAND

# PREFACE

Imagine yourself in a Thai temple with the sun's brightness reflected in countless glittering mosaic tiles, with contrasting and complementary colours combining to form a dazzling whole. The visitor to Thailand may be struck by many brilliant images, each reflecting an aspect of the country but none containing the whole picture. For Thailand, united by its long history of independence, a deep reverence and affection for its monarchy and respect for the Buddhist faith, is also a land of great variety and contrast.

In the mosaic you can find both an age-old pattern of farming life and one of the world's most modern skylines; traditional arts and skills preserved but also contemporary reinterpretations seen through modern eyes; remains of the artistry of ancient civilizations and a contemporary genius for the decorative arts, as expressed in splendid dance costumes, world-class jewellery and silks, and the intricately carved decorations found on Thai restaurant tables around the world.

It is no easy task to capture the spirit of Thailand in a book or short visit. Each region has something of its own to offer, from the treasures of marine life in the Andaman sea to internationally recognised World Heritage sites and National Parks. Just as Thailand opens its doors to welcome visitors to see for themselves its rich variety, so readers of *This Is Thailand*, whether familiar with the country or perhaps still contemplating their first visit, may, through some of the striking images from all parts of the country captured here on film and in prose, begin to see beyond the details to the bigger picture that makes this country so unique.

Seree Wangpaichitr
Governor
Tourism Authority of Thailand

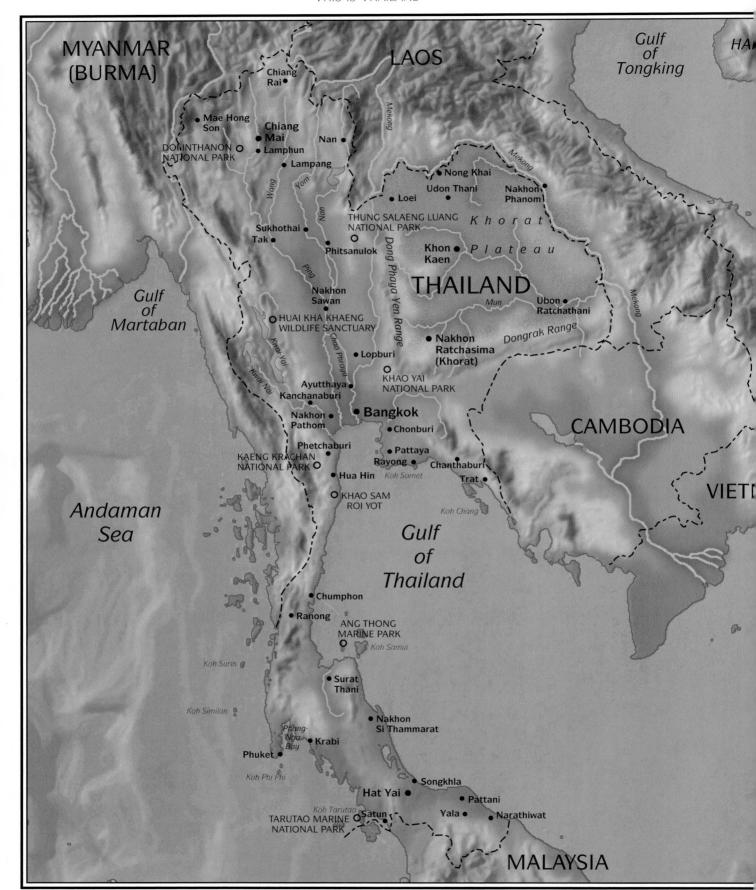

# PROFILE OF THAILAND

An elevated tollway leads from the airport into Bangkok, a stream of vehicles passing over a snarl of even more cars, buses and trucks on the highway beneath. The city's skyline bristles with high-rise offices, condominiums, luxury hotels and shopping plazas. Nothing seems to justify Thailand's popular reputation as the most exotic country in Asia. Then, as the taxi passes one of the busiest downtown intersections, the scene of urban chaos is fleetingly replaced by a glimpse of classical oriental wonder. There, on the street corner, is an ornate little shrine housing a gilded statue of the four-headed, eight-armed god Brahma. Devotees clutching smouldering sticks of incense make offerings, while elaborately costumed classical dancers weave slow, sinuous movements in an atmosphere heady with the scent of jasmine. It is a daily scene at the Erawan Shrine, which, regardless of the surrounding modern world, is still believed to be Thailand's most potent source of good fortune.

All countries are different but some are more different than others, and Thailand is happily and uniquely itself. Throughout 700 years of independence, the Thai Kingdom has displayed an amazing continuity, underpinned by the people's unwavering adherence to Buddhism, the national religion, and to the monarchy.

Thailand conjures in most minds striking images of golden spires and sweeping temple roofs, of emerald paddy fields, forested hills and elephants, of travel poster clichés depicting white sandy beaches fringed by palms. Such scenes are to be found, but popular conceptions give only part of the picture, and the land, its people and their history make up a complex nation with its own distinct characteristics.

As the 20th century draws to a close, Thailand is undergoing unprecedented growth and change as increasing prosperity, Westernization and a growing society of young urban professionals challenge the old ways without posing any clear alternatives. Cause for concern perhaps, but the most remarkable characteristic of the Thais has always been their resilience. It is all a balancing act, and the underlying quality of Thai-ness maintains the quintessential paradox of Thailand's Janus stance as it looks to the past with pride and to the future with confidence.

## THE LAND

What is an extraordinarily rich and diverse land arises from Thailand's geographical make up. Located within the latitudes 6 degrees and 21 degrees north, Thailand extends 1,650 kilometres (1,025 miles) north to south and 800 kilometres (500 miles) east to west. The shape of the country is extremely irregular – often fancifully likened to an elephant's head, with its trunk extending down to the Malay Peninsula — and produces a topographical range running from forested mountains and steep river valleys in the north to a long narrow southern peninsula with a coastline touched by both the Indian Ocean and the inshore extensions of the Pacific Ocean, and fringed with tropical beaches and offshore islands. Between these extremes lie the rich agricultural lands of central Thailand, while to the east is the semi-arid Khorat Plateau.

Situated in the heart of South-east Asia, the country occupies 513,115 square kilometres (198,114 square miles), an area roughly the size of France, and is bordered by Myanmar (Burma) in the west, Laos in the north-east, Cambodia in the east and Malaysia in the south. The landmass lies between two mountain systems – the Central Cordillera in the west and the Cordillera of Annam in the east – and divides into six topographical regions: the North, the Central Plains, the North-east, the South-east, the West and the Southern peninsula.

Northern Thailand, covering about one-quarter of the nation's area, is primarily a region of parallel mountain ranges running north to south and divided by steep, fertile river valleys. Most of the hills are between 500 and 1,000 metres (1,600–3,000 feet) in elevation, although five peaks rise over 2,000 metres (6,500 feet). Doi Inthanon, south of Chiang Mai, is the kingdom's highest mountain at 2,565 metres (8,415 feet). The lower hills are typically covered with deciduous forests, where teak was once dominant. However, excessive logging, combined with the slash-and-burn agriculture of the hilltribe people who have long inhabited the upland areas, has resulted in the serious depletion of forest cover. Above 1,000 metres (3,000 feet), the mountains support evergreen forests harbouring a wealth of plant and animal species.

The area forms a vital watershed region and in the mountains are the headwaters of four principal rivers, the Ping, Wang, Yom and Nan, which flow south to join the Chao Phraya river, Thailand's major waterway. Although most of the water run-off is to the south, the basins of the far north flow north-east to feed the Mekong river.

Directly below the northern region and extending 450 kilometres (290 miles) down to the Gulf of Thailand are the Central Plains, the nation's heartland. This characteristically flat region is dominated by the Chao Phraya river, which supports an extensive and highly developed network of canals and irrigation projects to form the kingdom's 'rice bowl'. Made intensely fertile by rich alluvial deposits, the countryside presents archetypal images of an exotic Asian land, typified by a patchwork of paddy fields, broken here and there by stands of palms between which glint the gilded spires and soaring roofs of village temples. The concentrated rural population of the Central Plains is startlingly contrasted at the region's south-eastern edge, at the head of the Gulf, where Bangkok, the hub of the nation's industrial and commercial activity, sprawls like an urban pancake.

A further marked contrast is found in the North-east, where the extensive Khorat Plateau rises some 300 metres (1,000 feet) above the Central Plains. The area covers about one-third of the country and is bounded in the south by the Dongrak mountains, which form the border with Cambodia, and on the west by the flat-topped Dong Phaya Yen mountains. Ringed by the Mekong river in the north and east, the region is essentially a large basin, drained by the Mun and other smaller tributaries of the Mekong.

Known as *I-san* in Thai, the North-east is the poorest and least developed part of the country, its economy scarcely rising above subsistence farming. A once dense cover of deciduous forest has been almost totally destroyed by man's encroachment, and much of the land is poor, subject to seasonal droughts and floods, while the soil is often salty. The landscape is not all bleak, however. Pockets of forest cover have survived due, ironically, to political insecurity in parts of the North-east, where strongholds of communist insurgency existed in the 1970s and where, in the 1980s and 1990s, Cambodian resistance forces have operated in the southern border areas.

Unlike I-san, the South-east has undergone dramatic change over the last two decades. The smallest of Thailand's topographical regions, forming a wedge of land between the Gulf of Thailand and the mountains of south-west Cambodia, the area comprises a narrow coastal plain backed by a hinterland of low hills. Traditionally, much of the land has been commercially produc-

Above: *Typical of northern Thailand's landscape are fertile valleys and forested mountains, here encircling Mae Hong Son.*

PREVIOUS PAGES
Page 10: *Elaborately costumed performers execute the graceful movements of the classical* lakon nai *dance drama.*
Page 11: *Thai children hold their hands in the* wai, *the traditional Thai greeting.*

*Rice fields cover much of Thailand's rural landscape in the North as well as in the Central Plains, the nation's rice bowl.*

*Off Thailand's southern peninsula lie numerous tropical islands, many, such as Koh Samui, edged with palm-fringed, white-sand beaches.*

tive, both in fresh produce, notably fruits and spices, and in sapphires and rubies mined in the south-easternmost provinces of Chanthaburi and Trat.

Today a new prosperity is taking over the area and what is now called the Eastern Seaboard has, since the mid-1980s, been extensively developed as an industrial and tourism zone, while the hinterland has been transformed by the construction of new highways giving access to Bangkok and to the North-east. Much of the indented coast-line is dotted with rocky offshore islands. Many of these are still forested, although some, like Koh Chang, are now being groomed as tourist resorts.

The West of Thailand, straddling the area between Bangkok and the Burmese border, forms a continuation of the northern mountains, although the valleys are smaller and the plains fewer. Several tributaries of the Chao Phraya and Salween rivers rise in the mountains, while the main river system is that of the Kwai Yai and Kwai Noi which join to form the Mae Khlong at Kanchanaburi, site of the infamous Bridge over the River Kwai built by allied POWs during World War II. In spite of tourism development in the valleys of the Kwai Yai and Kwai Noi, the West contains some of Thailand's richest surviving forest covers.

The last topographical region, the Southern peninsula, is a long sliver of land with a steep mountainous spine, a continuation of the western uplands and rising to more than 1,800 metres (5,900 feet). Extending from central Thailand down to the Malaysian border, the area is character-ized by sheer humped formations of lime-stone karst, which appear as both inland cliffs and offshore islets. The climate and habitat are close to those of the true rain-forest, and the flora and fauna are similar to those of Malaysia rather than the predomi-nantly Indo-Burmese varieties of the conti-nental lowlands. Rubber and coconut cultivation, as well as tin mining, are the tra-ditional economic activities of the region.

The western coast of the peninsula, bor-dered by the Andaman Sea, is very irregular and indented with estuaries and mangrove inlets. It is also strung with offshore islands, including Thailand's largest island, Phuket, connected to the mainland by a causeway. On the eastern shore, facing the Gulf of Thailand, are long stretches of beach.

## THE SEASONAL CYCLE

It has been a sunny June morning when, suddenly, in mid-afternoon dark clouds have gathered seemingly out of nowhere and with no more warning the heavens

open. Just a half-hour downpour during the rainy season and modern Bangkok trans-forms itself to mock its old soubriquet, 'Venice of the East', except it is no longer canals but flooded streets that criss-cross the city.

Low-lying on an alluvial plain, Bangkok is especially susceptible to flooding when the monsoon rains coincide with a high tide on the Chao Phraya river. Even modest rainfall can produce depressingly familiar scenes of watery weariness – office girls clutching their shoes and wading knee deep; shop-keepers piling sandbags across their door-ways; residents paddling sampans down side streets. Generally it is all accepted with good grace, and so it should be as Thailand has traditionally depended on, and pros-pered from, the annual rains.

An idea of just how vital the rains are is vividly illustrated by scenes of the semi-arid North-east during the hottest months of April and May. Earth, baked rock hard by the relentless sun, cracks and deep fissures pattern the land like fractured safety glass.

But too much or too little rain is relative, and while Thailand can be mildly uncom-fortable for brief moments of the year, the country is in the main extremely fortunate when compared to the drought-ridden or flood-devastated lands of other parts of

*During the rainy season, when the Buddhist Rains Retreat is celebrated, vivid green rice plants shoot up to form an emerald patchwork of paddy fields.*

held in May to ensure plentiful rains, are peculiar to specific regions.

As the earth softens with the early downpours, the soil, previously baked hard during the inactive hot season, yields to the plough, turning thick and moist. Mechanization has yet to alter the timeless scene, and although a few farmers may now use a small mechanical plough, the vast majority continue to rely on the strength of water buffalo. Once the fields have been prepared, the arduous task of transplanting rice seedlings begins. Working in lines, backs bent and heads covered with scarves and straw hats, men, women and children laboriously root the young plants in the flooded earth. Gradually the countryside assumes a brilliant hue as vivid green rice shoots carpet the land.

While the new crop slowly matures, the annual three-month Buddhist Rains Retreat is celebrated. It is a time when Buddhist monks remain in their monasteries, although the tradition predates Buddhism and is derived from ancient India, where itinerant holy men would pass the rainy season in permanent dwelling, lest in their wanderings they might inadvertently tread on freshly planted crops.

By the end of October, with the rains drawing to a close, the air cools and the paddy fields turn golden yellow as the rice ripens. The night of the full moon in November, before harvest time, is the occasion for the most enchanting of the festivals that punctuate the Thai year, *Loy Krathong.* The word *loy* means 'to float' and a *krathong* is a little lotus-shaped vessel made of banana leaves and containing flowers, incense sticks, a candle and a coin as offering to Mae Khongkha, goddess of rivers and waterways. By moonlight, people throughout the country, in Bangkok as well as in the tiniest village, gather on the banks of rivers, lakes and ponds to float their *krathongs* so that they may carry away the past year's sins, as well as send forth wishes for good fortune in the future.

In late November or early December, the rice crop is fully ripe and the year end is a busy time for the entire rural community, with everyone, young and old, toiling long hours to gather in the harvest. With the crop gathered and the stubble burnt off, an air of quiet tropical ease descends over vil-

Asia. It is totally free of virtually all the natural catastrophes suffered by its neighbours, the volcanic eruptions and perennial typhoons which wreak havoc in, for example, the Philippines.

The rhythm of the year is set by Thailand's tropical climate, which is dominated by alternating monsoons producing three seasons, although the climatic shifts are not necessarily appreciable to temperate-clime visitors, who tend to find the country hot and humid whatever the month. From the farmer's point of view, however,

these timely monsoonal changes are vital.

The south-west monsoon prevails from around June to mid-October and carries moisture from the Indian Ocean, producing the wet season which accounts for most of the country's average annual rainfall of 1,550 millimetres (60 inches). From mid-October to mid-February the wind shifts with the north-east monsoon bringing dry air from China and producing a so-called cool season. The third, hot, season comes in the months of March, April and May. The average annual temperature range is from 30°C (100°F) to 19°C (66°F).

The traditional Thai year dawns in the hottest month of April, New Year's Day falling on 13 April and marked by the *Songkran* Festival, when water is sprinkled over Buddha images as ritual of cleansing, and splashed over one and all in a less than spiritual mark of the festivities. But the seasonal cycle dictating the agricultural year more properly begins with the advent of the rains in late May or June.

Throughout, the cycle is punctuated by time-honoured ceremonies and festivals, which serve both as holidays from the toil of agricultural work and as rituals serving the ancient beliefs that underpin village life. Some occasions, such as the Ploughing Ceremony, are national affairs; others, such as the Rocket Festival in the North-east,

*The* Songkran *Festival celebrates the Thai New Year; passers-by are splashed, and often soaked, with water.*

*The flora of the Kingdom is as diverse as its fauna. With a rich variety of habitats in which to flourish, the flowering plants of Thailand range from the rhododendrons (right) of its northern mountains to the Lotus lilies (below right) of its lagoons and lakes. Off its tropical coasts lie the wonders of the underwater realm: a spectacular profusion of coral reefs (far right) and teeming marine life, including turtles, rays and even an occasional elusive Dugong.*

For size there is nothing to beat the python, with the Reticulated Python growing up to 10 metres (30 feet) or more. The other two species found in Thailand, the Blood Python and the Rock Python, are considerably smaller. Beautifully marked, they are handsome and immensely powerful snakes, that can strike with speed, suffocating their prey by constriction.

Of other snakes, and often the most startlingly beautiful, there are 14 species of vipers, 10 of which inhabit trees and can be glimpsed gliding through the branches in search of small lizards. Deadliest are the Russell's Viper and the Malayan Pit Viper, which account for the larger number of venomous snake bites.

Once as feared as snakes, the crocodile has fared less well in Thailand. Both the freshwater and the saltwater species are now all but locally extinct, having suffered from the hunter and from loss of habitat. Some may still exist in remote areas, but the only realistic chance of spotting the beast is at one of the crocodile farms near Bangkok, where the animals are reared for their skins, serving as tourist attractions before ending up as handbags and shoes.

Three species of the terrestrial tortoise make their home in Thailand, and are found in most areas except the marshy central plains. Freshwater turtles outside of temple ponds and pools are now rare and virtually all the 18 or so species found in Thailand are endangered. Giant marine turtles come to lay their eggs on the beaches of Thailand's southern shores during September to February. The largest of all is the Leatherback, weighing up to 900 kilograms (2,000 pounds). Ridley's Turtles and a few Green Turtles and Hawksbills are

also visitors to the southernmost shores.

Completing the reptilian and amphibian world are numerous species of frogs and toads, their croaks loudly punctuating the night air during the rainy season, and a great variety of lizards, ranging from the more than 2-metre (6-foot) long monitors to tiny skinks. So common as to be almost characteristic of the Thai home are the geckos. Not only useful in feeding on insects, the Common House Gecko, or *jingjok*, is an entertaining little creature, defying gravity with its adhesive toe pads which allow it to scuttle up smooth surfaces and across ceilings with ease.

Also familiar is the gecko known as a

tokay, so named for the sound of its distinctive deep-throated call. Fat and with its greyish skin mottled with blue and orange spots, it not as friendly-looking as the *jingjok*, but the Thais believe it is a lucky omen if its call is heard repeated nine times. It never is and the tokay rarely calls more than five times in succession.

### INSECTS

Nowhere is Thailand's rich natural diversity more apparent than in its insect life. Perhaps not the most obviously attractive of nature's realms – popularly considered as little more than a source of pests and irritating bites – the insect world is full of amazement and beauty that often goes unappreciated. Tropic nights, for example, would not be the same without the shrill rasping of the cicadas and the hypnotic sound of countless other insects.

No one can hazard a guess at precisely how many species of insects are found in Thailand, all that is certain is that many remain to be discovered. What is known, however, is staggering enough and, for example, there are an estimated 10,000 species of beetles, some 1,200 butterflies and close to 200 species of hawk moths. Thailand's butterflies outshine even birds in the beauty and brilliance of their colours, and on a stroll in a forest park many different species can be seen, fluttering gently in the air or clustered around some flowering shrub. As exotic as their looks are their names — windmills, swordtails, dragontails, courtesans, marquis and a host more.

## THE HISTORY OF THAILAND

### HISTORICAL INDEPENDENCE
Throughout its historical development Thailand, or Siam as it was known until well into the 20th century, has displayed marked continuity, compared to its neighbours, and is unique in the history of South-east Asia in that it was never colonized by a Western power – a fact in which the Thais take enormous pride. Although there was considerable European intervention during the development of the modern state, and Western models were followed in shaping political, social and economic institutions, Thailand is distinguished by certain historical traits and characteristics that have remained constant.

Primarily, the Thais have been rice cultivators and devout Buddhists, content to leave government in the hands of an educated élite. The social order has been hierarchical, based on wealth, status and influence; maintaining the equilibrium was an acceptance of the obligations of status and the reciprocation of services rendered.

The nation's cultural, social and political roots can be traced back centuries to the early Thai kingdoms, and the idea of the past – in which myth and legend are mixed with historical fact – has served to sustain national identity in spite of borrowings from regional predecessors as well as from the West. This identity has three symbolic foundations in the monarchy, Buddhism and nationhood, the first two in particular being quintessential to an understanding of Thailand's history.

### PREHISTORY
Located on the migratory route from southern China, Thailand has attracted

*Excavations at Ban Chiang revealed a wealth of painted pottery, evidence of a flourishing prehistoric culture.*

diverse peoples since prehistoric times. Ample archaeological evidence suggests the existence of a thriving Paleolithic culture in the region, which has probably supported continuous human habitation for at least 20,000 years.

Thailand's original inhabitants were likely to have been non-Mongoloid peoples, perhaps Negritos or Polynesians. While little is known about these earliest settlers, excavations conducted in the 1970s at Ban Chiang in north-eastern Thailand indicate an advanced culture flourishing in the area as far back as 3600 BC.

It would appear that the land was first populated by diverse waves of immigration, attracted to the area by the fertility of the land, most especially the Chao Phraya river basin. By the end of the first millennium BC, tribal territories in peninsular South-east Asia had begun to coalesce into protohistorical kingdoms, the earliest of which was Funan, centred on the Mekong Delta, now part of Vietnam. Ultimately, through a steady and prolonged migration, the Thais entered the region from their original homeland in southern China, and eventually rose to become the dominant force in the peninsula. Prior to their ascendancy, however, various influences were at work, establishing a pattern of civilization to which the Thais became cultural heirs.

### EARLY KINGDOMS
Fundamental to the cultural development of the entire Indochina peninsula was the impact of ancient India. Social, religious and artistic roots can all be traced back to this shaping force. In the first centuries AD Indian traders were crossing the Bay of Bengal and venturing into the Far East. Because of the types of ships they sailed and the prevailing seasonal monsoons, their journeys east and south required stops at ports along the Indochina peninsula. During these sojourns a process of Indianization very gradually took place. The merchants themselves probably had little lasting impact on the indigenous cultures and it was more likely that Indian princes set themselves up to rule over petty states, marrying into the local population to legitimize their authority.

The process of Indianization formed a cultural base out of which developed a number of independent kingdoms in the centuries before the rise of the Thai. Three, in particular, were especially formative on what would later become Thailand.

The first of these, Dvaravati, was a vaguely united group of Mon people, who had entered the region probably from southern China and settled in a collection of city states with, most likely, a power base at what is now Nakhon Pathom, west of beings who declined entering *nirvana* in order to help others.

Buddhism was first introduced to the region that is now Thailand in the 3rd century BC when, according to tradition, the Indian emperor Ashoka sent two missionaries to the 'Land of Gold'. This has been tentatively identified as the Mon kingdom of Dvaravati centred on the modern town of Nakhon Pathom, west of Bangkok.

By the time of the founding of the first Thai sovereign state at Sukhothai in the early 13th century, Buddhist monks in the southern part of the country had made contact with Sri Lanka. From there came the doctrine of Theravada Buddhism based on Pali texts, as opposed to the Sanskrit scriptures of Mahayana.

Today, Thailand supports a religious community of some 250,000 monks who reside at an estimated 27,000 temple monasteries throughout the country. The monastic system is central to Theravada Buddhism and, aside from a core religious community, most monks are ordained for only a short spell, perhaps just a few days but more usually the three months of the Buddhist Rains Retreat. As in the past, young Thai men become monks temporarily to earn merit for their parents as well as for their own spiritual development.

In trying to lead a good life the layman, too, has the opportunity to accrue merit which will ensure rebirth under more favourable conditions in the next incarnation. Ways in which lay people may earn merit are many and various. Most typical and most visible is giving food and other offerings to monks who make early morning alms rounds in cities, towns, and villages throughout the country.

### OTHER RELIGIONS

Although Thais are overwhelmingly Buddhist, they are a tolerant people and other religions coexist with the national faith. Muslims comprise Thailand's largest religious minority, numbering about 2 million, or roughly 4 per cent of the population. Islam was reputedly introduced into the region in the 13th century by Arab traders calling at ports along the Malay peninsula, and most Thai Muslims are of Malay descent, living primarily in the southernmost provinces of Narathiwat, Pattani, Yala and Satun. Aside from Thailand's approximately 2,000 mosques and some 200 Muslim schools, freedom to practise the faith is witnessed in many ways and, for example, government employees are allowed leave to attend major festivals, as well as to make the Haj pilgrimage.

A further 1 per cent of Thailand's population is made up of Christians, Taoists, Mahayana Buddhists, Confucianists, Hindus and Sikhs. The practice of these faiths largely follows ethnic patterns, and there have been comparatively few Thai converts. Ethnic Chinese and Vietnamese account for most of the Christians, Taoists, Mahayana Buddhists and Confucianists, while Hindus and Sikhs belong mainly to Bangkok's sizeable Indian community.

While other minority religions owe their presence primarily to migration, Christianity was brought to Thailand by missionaries. First, in the 16th and 17th centuries, came Dominicans, Franciscans and Jesuits from Spain and Portugal, and later they were joined by their Protestant counterparts, Presbyterians, Baptists and Seventh-Day Adventists. In spite of making few converts among the Thais, Christianity has had a significant impact, especially in education and medicine. Many local schools and hospitals are Christian affiliated, while Western surgery, vaccination and other medical practices were first introduced by Christians.

### THE SUPERNATURAL

Pervasive and genuine though their adherence to Buddhism is, the Thais have inherited from their ancestors animistic practices which interact with ordinary life. These include beliefs in charms, amulets, magical tattoos, fortune-telling, exorcism and other shamanistic rituals, as well as in spirits.

Buddhism, in placing ultimate responsibility for salvation firmly on each individual, does not address in any practical way people's fears and hopes as encountered in day-to-day life. Accordingly, the Thais have retained a host of ancient beliefs in supernatural forces which are thought to be capable of influencing and exerting power over the events of daily life. The beliefs originated with the human mind's attempt to cope with the uncontrollable crises of mundane existence – accidents, natural disasters, disease and other sources of fear and insecurity.

*Robed in white, to represent purity, and bearing a traditional offering, a young man is carried, shoulder-high, to the temple for his ordination as a monk.*

Perhaps the most widespread and easily seen manifestations of supernatural beliefs are spirit houses. Found in the compounds of virtually every home, business premises, government office and public building, these are ornate model dwellings designed in the form of temples or traditional-style Thai houses. Commonly raised on a short column, they are usually garlanded with flowers and often provided with food offerings. Their presence stems from a belief that spirits inhabited the site before humans settled in and, lest they should become angered and bring misfortune, they must be placated by the provision of a home of their own.

More troublesome than the spirits inhabiting a compound are others which can take possession of a person's body. To combat these there is a variety of shamans and exorcists, mostly lay people but sometimes monks, who are renowned for having power over malevolent *phi,* or spirits.

The act of exorcism differs from shaman to shaman. Some are extremely theatrical, favouring elaborate costumes and wielding swords and knives in their struggle to wrest the spirit from the body of the possessed. Others are less dramatic and generally employ the elements of fire and water, waving a bunch of lighted candles and sprinkling the affected subject with water.

Closely allied to exorcists are mediums, people, often women, capable of going into a trance and allowing themselves to become possessed by a benevolent spirit. Under this influence they are able to perform acts of healing and similar services.

While shamans and mediums perform a curative function, tattoos and amulets play a prophylactic role in supernatural belief. Both are thought to bestow invulnerability from all kinds of weapons, also to protect against snake bites, as well as to give the power of attracting admiration and love.

Tattoo designs are typically animals (double-tailed lizards are popular), figures from classical Thai mythology or magic spells written in ancient Khmer script. Amulets can be all manner of things. Most common are images of the Buddha or some highly revered monk. However, as amulets long pre-date Buddhism, and were initially rare objects found in nature – a hollow tiger's tooth, for example – many have no religious association. Popular among these are wooden phalluses, *palad khik,* and small rolls of gilded metal containing a magic inscription, *takrud.*

The important thing about both tattoos and amulets is that they have no protective power in themselves, or that their power is dormant unless activated. Thus amulets must be blessed, and tattoos have a spell cast over them by the tattooist. After completing a tattoo and chanting a magic spell to imbue it with power, the tattooist will proffer moral advice. Should the tattooee not follow this and commit some sin, the power of the tattoo can be diminished or completely destroyed.

One major difference between amulets and tattoos today is that something of a social stigma is attached to the latter. Because of this some tattoos are executed in invisible ink, made from sesame oil, so the wearer may have the protective benefit without the visual marks.

## FOOD AND DRINK

As an ever-growing number of restaurants around the world attest, Thai cuisine today enjoys unprecedented popularity among lovers of good food. Its distinctive blend of flavours and ingredients make it quite different from anything else in Asia.

The basis of a Thai meal is, of course, rice. This is commonly steamed, although it may be made into noodles, while glutinous or 'sticky' rice is preferred with some regional specialities. Accompanying are four or five main dishes featuring vegetables, meat, seafood, fish, egg and soup.

Besides the rice and main dishes, absolutely essential to any Thai meal are the sauces to give additional spice and seasoning. For the novice there can be a bewildering number of these, but the most common are *nam pla,* a liquid fish sauce which is extremely salty, and *nam prik,* also a liquid but with pieces of chillies, garlic, shrimp curd, sugar and lime.

Although Thais generally prefer hot, spicy food, it is a misconception that all Thai dishes are equally fiery. There are grades of hotness, and hence the array of sauces to adjust seasoning according to preference. However, much of the appeal of Thai cuisine is derived from its seasoning. Red and green chillies of a dozen kinds are but some of many different ingredients that are combined to give a unique blend of flavours. Lemon grass, garlic, ginger, nutmeg, cloves coriander, turmeric and other herbs and spices all have a role to play.

Another crucial element is the prepara-

*Spirit houses, here displayed for sale, are found in the vicinity of almost every home and business throughout the country.*

tion of ingredients. Thai cooks are expert in the handling of tools and skilled at slicing, cutting and carving vegetables, fruit and meats. The practice of carving food items in delicate and intricate patterns, as well as in figurative forms such as boats, fish, ornamental jars and so on, has a long tradition in Thailand. In former times this was primarily a speciality of the women at the royal court, who would turn cucumbers, papayas, tomatoes, carrots, radishes, onions and other prosaic foods into exquisite works of art fit to decorate a king's banquet table.

A further consideration for the Thai cook is time. The preparation of a Thai dinner can take all day, starting in the early morning with shopping at the local market for the day's freshest and best buys. Then the spices must be prepared anew for each meal, and ground painstakingly to ensure the perfect blend and the fullest flavour.

And so to the individual types of dishes. In the soup department, Thailand's great contribution to the culinary arts is *tom yam*. This is a sour soup which can be made with various kinds of meat or fish, but its most famous version is with prawns (*tom yam goong*). The basic broth is flavoured with lemon grass, citrus leaves, lime juice, fish sauce and hot chillies.

Other common methods of Thai food preparation include curries (*gaeng*), usually hot and spicy, and the stir-fried dishes which are cooked in a wok with pork fat oil, pepper and plenty of garlic. Then there is a wide choice of salad preparations (*yam*) made with just vegetables or with different kinds of meat or fish mixed with distinctive flavourings such as lemon grass, fish sauce and such like, plus lime juice to give a characteristic sourness. For dessert there are many sorts of local sweets (*kanom*) often of a coconut flavour, and a vast choice of tropical fruits from the common-or-garden pineapples and banana (numerous varieties) to exotic discoveries like the hairy rambutan and the tasty durian.

In addition to standard Thai dishes there are many regional specialities. In the North, for example, glutinous rather than plain rice is the typical staple, while curries tend to be thinner, made without the coconut milk favoured in central and southern Thailand. The northern region's proximity to neighbouring Myanmar (Burma) also accounts for

*Thai food, especially 'royal' Thai cuisine, is as beautifully presented as it is delicious. Carving fruit and vegetables into intricate shapes is one of the most traditional – and impressive – presentation techniques.*

some distinct dishes, such as *gaeng hang lay*, a pork curry seasoned with ginger, turmeric and tamarind.

North-eastern Thailand possesses a regional cuisine that has become extremely popular in recent years. It features a wide variety of exotic ingredients, among them frogs and grasshoppers, and uses chilli peppers to a greater degree than elsewhere in Thailand. Among typical north-eastern dishes often seen on menus today are green papaya salad (*som tam*) and spicy minced meat or chicken known as *laab*.

In the South, cooking tends to be dominated by two local ingredients found in abundance: seafood and coconut. Fish and shellfish caught off the southern shores appear more widely on menus than meat or poultry, while the coconut provides milk for thickening soups and curries, oil for frying and grated coconut meat which is used as a condiment. Cultural influences also play a part, as witnessed in Indian style curries and Indonesian *satays*.

For drinks, beer is a good (though comparatively expensive) complement to Thai food. Typically Thai are various local spirits of which 'Mekong' rice whisky is the most famous. Distilled from molasses and sticky rice in a month-long

process, 'Mekong' has a slightly coarse flavour which is an acquired taste.

## SPORTS AND ENTERTAINMENT

The pervading lifestyle is strongly influenced by the Thais' particular talent for enjoyment, having a good time – *sanuk*, as it is in Thai. All languages have some words that cannot be perfectly translated because they embrace something special about the culture. *Sanuk* is the unique Thai word that means, more or less, 'to be fun' and *sanuk* is found in all things from organized entertainment to eating or simply taking a walk; *pai teeo*, roughly translating as 'taking a stroll', is the standard response to the question of 'where are you going' asked on a chance encounter in the street.

In the wake of the nation's rapid modernization and Westernization, today's Thais like to play golf, go to the cinema and eat hamburgers and fries. But even in pursuing these alien activities the people display an essentially Thai delight in anything that is new, different, novel. Golf is given a typically Thai sybaritic touch. New courses are landscaped by the dozen, clubhouses are luxurious, and caddies, usually young girls, are so cheap that a golfer may hire several, one to carry clubs, one to hold an umbrella, one to spot to the ball, one to fetch drinks and perhaps another to offer consolation at a sliced shot.

None the less traditional sports and pastimes still persist. Kick boxing (*Muay Thai*) remains Thailand's most popular spectator sport. Developed from an ancient style of martial art, *Muay Thai* differs from ordinary boxing in using the feet, knees and elbows as weapons in addition to gloved fists. At its best it is a fast and furious contest between two superbly fit athletes. Often as entertaining as the fight are the spectators who variously shout encouragement, yell abuse and gesticulate madly as bets are made across the crowded arena.

Other violent sports are Thai sword fighting (*krabi-krabong*), and improbable animal contests: bull fighting (a southern Thai speciality in which bull is pitted against bull), fish fighting, cock fighting (illegal) and even beetle fighting (two males are placed on a bamboo stick in which a female has been trapped and are made to fight for the honour).

Also very Thai but far less violent is *takraw*, a game somewhat akin to volleyball in which a rattan ball is knocked around by using the feet, legs and head only. A recognized sport at national and regional meets, *takraw* is, however, most commonly seen being played by young labourers during their lunch break on any open space

Popular with young and old alike is kite-flying, from February to May. Colourful little paper creations fill Thai skies at this time, but kite flying is also a sport, a contest in which huge *chula* 'masculine' kites try to bring down smaller *pakpao* 'female' kites.

# THE VISUAL ARTS

### ARCHITECTURE

Two traditional building forms define the architecture of Thailand: the Buddhist temple (from which royal and ceremonial architecture was also derived) and the teakwood

*Kick boxing contests are exciting events. The pace is fast, the atmosphere charged and the noise loud. The contestants' most lethal weapons are their feet, which can be used against all parts of the body.*

house. Both forms depend very largely on an architecture of the roof, with buildings being essentially post-and-beam structures supporting steeply angled, multi-tiered roofs with overhanging eaves. The basic design originates from Chinese architecture, which had a strong influence on East Asia in much the same way as ancient Greece can be said to have 'invented' architecture for the West.

Created to impart a sense of reverence and serenity, the Thai Buddhist temple is in essence a harmonious arrangement of simple horizontal masses and highly decorated vertical forms. To describe the architecture as a 'temple' is somewhat misleading as the label, implying a single structure, like a Christian church, is an unsatisfactory trans-

lation of the Thai word *wat*, which refers to a temple/monastery complex comprising several distinct religious buildings, in addition to monks' residential quarters.

The principal structure is the *bot*, the most sacred part of the temple and the place where ordination ceremonies are conducted. The building is identified by eight boundary stones, called *sima*, placed outside at the four corners and the four cardinal points. A temple is also likely to have one or more *viharn*, a building used as a sermon hall for monks and lay worshippers.

Architecturally, the *bot* and *viharn* are virtually identical, being rectangular buildings with sweeping roofs covered with glazed tiles. Each end of the roof's peak terminates in a gilded finial known as a *cho fa*, or 'sky tassel'. A gracefully curved ornamentation, it looks like a slender bird's neck and head, and is generally believed to represent the mythical Garuda, half bird, half man.

Another characteristic of temple structures is the *chedi* or *stupa*. Dominating the compound of a *wat*, this is a tall decorative spire constructed over relics of the Buddha, sacred texts or an image. Essentially there are two basic forms: bell-shaped and raised on square or round terraces of diminishing size, and tapering to a thin spire; or a round, finger-like tower. The latter, derived from Khmer architecture and symbolic of the mythical mountain abode of the gods, is known as a *prang*.

Other buildings in a temple compound can include a library for sacred texts, and a *mondop*, a square-shaped building with tapering roof enshrining some relic, often a Buddha footprint, a stone impression far larger than life-size. Some larger *wats* may also have cloisters, open-sided galleries perhaps displaying rows of Buddha images, while bell towers and pavilions can be additional features. *Wats* further have a crematorium, identified by its needle-like chimney and, usually, a school for monks and perhaps also for lay children.

Rather like a medieval Christian church, the Thai temple was the focal point of every village. Unlike the church, however, it served far more than the community's spiritual needs. In the past, and still today in some rural areas, cultural life revolved around the *wat* which stood as social services centre, school, hospital, dispensary, hostelry, and village news, employment and information agency.

The earliest Thai temple buildings were strongly influenced by Khmer architecture with, for example, sandstone being used for door posts, lintels and rectangular windows. Later, from around the 12th century, brick replaced sandstone, the surface being finished with a stucco covering. But more characteristic than the materials is the ornamental decoration of Thai temples.

Probably initially derived from Chinese examples, Thai temple ornamentation is profuse, polychromatic and richly detailed. Roofs are tiled in orange and green, gables and spires are gilded, coloured glass mosaic adorns pediments and pillars. No surface is left unadorned and a remarkable array of techniques and materials are brought into play – woodcarving, stucco relief, lacquer, gilt, mother-of-pearl inlay, gold leaf and porcelain fragments. It all sounds far too much, but surprisingly such a seeming excess of ornamentation succeeds and the greatest achievement of the most traditional form of Thai architecture has been the decorative, not the monumental.

Domestic architecture is less obviously derivative of other cultures and less flamboyant than the temple. The traditional

teakwood house tries to blend typical Thai characteristics of grace and pragmatism.

A vital distinction of Thai-style houses is that they were intended to be portable. In the past when people moved house, they did literally that. Posts and panels would be carted off and re-assembled at a new site, a task that could be accomplished in a single day with the help of neighbours.

As prefabricated structures, Thai houses have walls of movable panels, frequently made in standard sizes so as to be interchangeable. These are assembled on site and are attached to a superstructure of sturdy columns and beams. Holding everything together are wooden pegs, non-wooden elements being rare in traditional Thai houses.

Roofs, covered with either wooden or ceramic tiles, are steeply sloped and given

*The bell-shaped* chedi's *supremely elegant proportions are exemplified by Sukhothai's Wat Sra Sri (above); the* prang, *a different type of* chedi, *found full expression at Ayutthaya (above, far right).*

*Sweeping temple roofs are most often tiled in orange and green, as at Bangkok's Wat Arun (above, centre). 'Sky tassels',* cho fa, *top all gable peaks while bargeboards, as at Wat Phra That Haripunchai, Lamphun (right), are intricately carved and decorated.*

a broad overhang to provide protection from the bright sunlight and the monsoon rains. There may also be a second, stepped roof level to facilitate ventilation.

Frequently located by a river or canal, the entire house is raised a couple of metres off the ground on sturdy pillars so as to give protection from floods and from snakes and other wild animals, as well as to allow air circulation. In former times, the ground floor space also provided sleeping quarters for the family's livestock.

Completing the basic design is a verandah. This is an integral element in a dwelling where almost half the space is set aside for outdoor living, and apart from affording a shady spot for escaping the worst heat of the day, the verandah can be turned into a kitchen garden with potted plants, a welcome convenience in times of floods.

Thai-style houses may be simple or complex. The essential unit is a rectangle some 3.5 by 9 metres (11 x 30 feet), the interior providing one or two rooms, but the living area can be easily enlarged with the addition of further units. As many as eight or ten components, arranged around an open central platform, can be integrated to produce one large dwelling sufficient to accommodate the extended family.

Besides the temple and the teakwood house, the only other local architecture of note is the shophouse, or *hong thaew* (literally 'room row'), which was the most ubiquitous secular building during the early years of modern commercial development. A shophouse, or rowshop, is precisely what the name implies, one of a row of shops with a simple but supremely functional design. Each unit is basically an oblong box, one room wide and three or four storeys high. The ground floor is used for commercial purposes – a shop, a restaurant, a workshop, warehouse or whatever – while the upper floors provide living quarters for the owner of the business and his family. Making its first appearance in Bangkok around the middle of the 19th century, the shophouse was the standard structure for building expansion in virtually every city and town in the country, until very recently.

Today, in the wake of rapid economic development, Bangkok and, to a lesser degree other big cities, display the now familiar pattern of post-modern international architecture — high-rises with glass curtain walls, office towers, condominiums, luxury hotels, shopping malls and housing estates. Bangkok in particular presents a fruit salad of architectural styles, from Classical Greek to Post Modern. House designs may range from a Roman villa to mock-Tudor, or a condominium can be bizarrely modelled on a Gothic cathedral.

## SCULPTURE

Virtually all classical Thai fine art is religious art, produced in the service of Buddhism, and sculpture is primarily the art of fashioning Buddha images in a profusion and beauty of form that are unmatched. More than any other type of art work, Buddha sculptures exemplify the Kingdom's aesthetic achievement and link 13 centuries of tradition which have moulded the artistic development of the land.

In this there is a curious irony. While Thai Buddha statues display high aesthetic standards and meticulous workmanship, the image has never been conceived nor perceived as a work of art. In their commissioning and fashioning, images were viewed as objects of devotion whose creation was an act of merit-making, not of self-expression.

There have been many shifting emphases in influence and style but, at the same time, artists were kept to strict guidelines and had to reproduce certain features and attitudes that were traditional and accepted as integral. Accordingly all images possess certain common features.

Firstly, the Buddha, as the Great Teacher, is represented as a human being,

*Traditional Thai houses were designed for portability; many fine examples from different regions are now located in Bangkok. The classic teak Kamthieng House (above), set in the grounds of the Siam Society, is from the North; from near Ayutthaya and other areas came the delightful pavilions (left), now preserved in the garden of the Suan Pakkard Palace .*

performance demands a vast cast of actors playing the roles of gods, giants, men, monkey warriors and assorted beasts. All the characters were at one time depicted by the actors wearing elaborate masks, but in latter-day shows only the masks of giants and animals have been retained. Nevertheless, any narrative is still left to a chorus, and actors keep their faces expressionless, communicating solely through a complex vocabulary of hand gestures and body movements.

*Lakon nai* may take its narrative content from a variety of legends, the *Inaw*, another princely tale, being one of the most popular. Masks are not worn by the dancers.

Traditionally, *lakon nai* was danced exclusively by women and *khon* only by men. Such a division between the sexes is no longer strictly adhered to, but it does point to a more vital distinction between the two dramatic styles. While both rely on gesture and posture as modes of expressing emotion as well as action, the *khon* actor seeks virtuosity in strength and agility and muscular exertion, the *lakon nai* dancer is persuasive through grace and remarkably controlled movement.

Serving as a counterpoint to the control and restraint of the dance itself are the costumes which are extremely rich and flamboyant. Made of intricately embroidered cloth, a leading male attire comprises a tight-fitting jacket, breeches and a loin cloth worn outside and held in place by a broad sash and a bejewelled belt. Ornaments such as bracelets, armlets and rings add further to a picture of sartorial splendour. For female players the typical dress is a long skirt and cape, pointed golden headdress and other jewellery that rivals if not surpasses the glory of the male.

Dancers do not wear make-up as in the Western theatrical tradition, where it is used to alter appearance to a greater or lesser extent, and instead facial features are merely accentuated in the usual manner. The *khon* masks are similarly conventional in the way that they depend on

colour symbolism and stylized design to depict the various characters, rather than make any attempt to portray the life-like.

Music is integral to all forms of Thai dance drama and performances are accompanied by an orchestra comprising traditional instruments, usually five percussion pieces and one woodwind. Small bell-like cymbals are used to set the pace while the music of the rest of the orchestra lends mood. Like most other aspects of classical

*Sinuous, graceful movements and gestures, especially of the arms and hands, characterize the* lakon nai *form of classical dance drama.*

Thai theatre, the orchestra is bound by convention. Essentially the tunes are indicative of specific actions and emotions, so there are 'walking tunes', 'marching tunes', 'laughing tunes', 'weeping tunes', 'anger tunes' and so on. Such passages are instantly recognizable by an audience accustomed to Thai musical notation and composition.

If *khon* and *lakon nai* can be compared as art to western ballet, *likay* is the equivalent of pantomime. The dramatic content is standard, full of the tried and tested stuff of melodrama – crossed lovers, maidens in distress, lost princes finally reunited with

their patrimony, and so forth. Improvisation, however, plays an important part, and one performance can differ markedly from another depending on the actors' quick wits and fertile sense of humour. Puns, verbal virtuosity and slapstick humour are *likay*'s stock-in-trade.

Costumes are allowed to run riot and there is a tendency for gaudy jewellery, grossly accentuated make-up, bright colours and generally raffish dress. Together it amounts to, as one commentator has remarked, 'imaginative bad taste'.

## LITERATURE

Thailand's literary tradition consists largely of mythological and historical fables. The majority of these are of Indian origin, but they have been so extensively revised and rewritten to suit local tastes and ideas as to become to all intents and purposes uniquely Thai in style and content.

The most famous tale of all, and one which has had an all-pervading influence on Thai classical arts, is the *Ramakien*, the Thai version of the Indian allegorical epic, the *Ramayana*. A moral tale concerning the struggles of Prince Rama and Hanuman's monkey army against the forces of evil, the saga opens with the founding of the rival cities of Ayutthaya, capital of the gods, and Langka, city of the demons. In what is a long and convoluted narrative, the principal action is episodic and focuses on the trials and tribulations of Ayutthaya's Prince Rama, the abduction of his wife, Sita, and the eventual defeat of Langka by Hanuman and his army of monkey warriors.

Reputedly written some 2,000 years ago and accredited to the Indian poet Valmiki, the *Ramakien* was early on incorporated, in one form or another, into the cultures of almost all South-east Asian civilizations, and was firmly established before the rise of the Thai kingdom. But early Thai versions were lost during the sack of Ayutthaya by the Burmese in 1767, and the fullest of the existing texts was written in 1807 by King Rama I, assisted by court poets.

Further royal patronage of the Thai literary tradition includes two episodes of the *Ramakien* which King Rama II composed for classical dance drama, the most common medium, along with the visual arts, in which the epic found expression. Other literary compositions by King Rama II include several epic poems – the best known being the *Inaw*, a romance with a Javanese background, although full of details illustrating Thai customs, habits and manners, as well as historical information. The monarch also collaborated with court poets, the finest of whom was Sunthorn Phu (1786–1855), widely regarded as Thailand's greatest literary figure. His highest achievement was to write supremely well in ordinary language, rather than in the courtly style, and thus appeal to all classes. His best known work, which has become a Thai classic, is *Phra Aphai Mani*, a romantic adventure concerning the odyssey of an exiled prince.

Popular literature throughout Thai history has had an oral rather than a written tradition, with well-known and well-loved tales transmitted by village storytellers. Legends, anecdotes and adventure yarns abound, although perhaps the most popular tales to survive are those concerning a peasant-born trickster known as Sri Thanonchai, whose numerous, often bizarre and hilarious escapades are played out largely against the background of medieval court life. The stories' timeless appeal, however, springs from Sri Thanonchai's endearing combination of cunning insolence and acute native wit which he employs to full effect in constant brushes with officialdom. As in many popular tales, humour, often earthy and bawdy, is a common element.

In the field of non-fiction, palm-leaf and paper manuscripts were widely produced. Because of the fragile medium, however, few surviving examples predate the 18th century. Written on long concertina-folded pages and often accompanied by beautifully painted illustrations, manuscripts covered the whole gamut of knowledge from religious texts to treatises on such diverse

*Many examples of traditional Thai craftsmanship can be seen at Wat Phra Keo, Bangkok. Here, mythological demons, known as* yaksha, *guard a golden* chedi.

subjects as elephant care, herbal medicine and military strategy.

Today, modern literature remains robust, particularly poetry which has always been a major art form; the Thais have an acute ear and great love for puns, play on words and verbal dexterity in general. There is also a considerable output of short stories and novels. Best known among the modern classics are probably the novels of the late elder statesman and former prime minister M.R. Kukrit Pramoj, whose major work, *Si Phandin* ('Four Reigns'), is set against the background of courtly life during the reigns of Kings Rama V to Rama VIII.

## CRAFTS

The Thais are adept at numerous crafts, their techniques handed down from generation to generation. Some, like silk and cotton weaving, have been long-held occupations of country folk, with production initially for domestic use until the later creation of commercial markets.

Most visible of the local craft traditions are the decorative arts, for which the Thais

possess a true genius. These range from the woodcarving and coloured glass mosaic used in the external decoration of temples, to black lacquer-and-gilt inlay work and mother-of-pearl inlay, both employed in furniture (manuscript cabinets, for example), doors and other flat surfaces.

Among handicrafts, the most famous today is hand-woven Thai silk. Produced in countless colours and designs, Thai silk was customarily used for clothing, but with the advent of mass-produced dress, the craft was in danger of dying out until it was revived in the 1950s as a commercial product, largely due to the efforts of the American entrepreneur, Jim Thompson. One of the best places for visitors to buy high-quality silks is at the Silk Company shop in Bangkok, near Thompson's beautiful teak house, now a museum. Today, Thai silk is woven in heavier weights ideal for draperies, upholstery and other household furnishing, while the rich fabric is further used for place mats and napkins, scarves and other accessories.

The most highly-prized of the traditional silks is a form known as *mat mee*, a fabric unique to north-east Thailand. Produced from tie-dyed silk threads, the fabric is hand-woven in a variety of beautiful designs, typically distinguished by intricate patterns and subtle colours. Once a neglected craft, *mat mee* silk has been revitalized in recent years through rural development projects initiated by Her Majesty Queen Sirikit. Today, the fabric enjoys an unprecedented vogue as a fashion material favoured by Her Majesty and other members of the Royal Family.

Of note among a host of other handicrafts — beaten silverware, lacquerware, basketry, paper umbrellas, rattan and wicker furniture — is nielloware. Practised in southern Thailand for hundreds of years, this is the craft of decorating gold and silver objects with delicate etched designs filled with a metal alloy. Workmanship of high quality is found in various objects, such as trays, boxes and vases.

Koh Phi Phi is one of the world's most beautiful island groups, although tourism development has caused some degradation of the marine environment. Khao Phanom Bencha is small — just 50 square kilometres (20 square miles) — but is a key conservation area, its rainforest supporting 156 bird species and 32 types of mammals.

**Surat Thani** Facing the Gulf of Thailand, Surat Thani is the largest province in the South. The area once formed part — and may have been the centre — of the Mahayana Buddhist Srivijaya empire (8th–13th centuries). Finds from the archaeological site of Chaiya, of which the best pieces are now displayed in Bangkok's National Museum, indicate cultural achievement of a high order. Historical interest is lacking in Surat Thani town, and the attraction of this commercial centre and port, supported by trade in rubber and coconut, lies in its typical southern character. The place is also the ferry point for Koh Samui, Thailand's third largest island (247 square kilometres/95 square miles) and now a beach destination rivalling Phuket in popularity. Ang Thong National Marine Park, comprising an archipelago of some 40 islands north-west of Samui, and Khao Sok National Park, on the mainland, are important conservation areas, the latter being one of the places in the country where tigers possibly still exist.

**Nakhon Si Thammarat** The provincial capital of Nakhon Si Thammarat, the South's second largest city (after Hat Yai), is the cultural heart of the region. Originally known as Ligor, the town dates back to the 2nd century AD and subsequently gained importance as a staging post on the early trade route between China and southern India. It was through Nakhon Si Thammarat that Theravada Buddhism spread from Sri Lanka to Sukhothai in the 13th century, and the place remains a major religious centre, the reputedly 1,000-year-old Wat Phra Mahathat being one of the South's most revered temples. Various regional arts and crafts, such as shadow puppets and niel-

loware (alloy inlaid in silver or gold objects), also continue to flourish here. Aside from the eastern coastline, the province is mountainous and forested, and the 570-square-kilometre (220-square-mile) Khao Luang National Park, encompassing the peninsula's highest peak (1,835 metres/6,020 feet), provides habitats for some 200 bird, 90 mammal and 31 reptile species.

**Phattalung** From mountains, forests and high plateau in the west, the eastern side of Phattalung slopes down to the upper shores of Songkhla Lake. Thale Noi Waterbird Sanctuary, a large lagoon which connects to the lake, is a protected area for 182 species of waterbird. Culturally, Phattalung

*The people of Narathiwat, Thailand's most southern province, are largely Muslim. Mosques and minarets attest to their cultural links with neighbouring Malaysia.*

is distinguished as the original home of two famous southern entertainments, *Manhora* dance and Thai shadow play.

**Songkhla** The province had the odd distinction of its administrative capital not being the major town. The brash and bustling commercial centre of Hat Yai, the South's business and communications hub, has that distinction, but Songkhla town is

the more interesting. Today a small, relaxed coastal resort located on a peninsula between the sea and the southern end of Songkhla lake, the town dates back to the 8th century and has a long history as a trading port, the legacy of which survives in traces of old architecture and a population mix of Thai, Chinese and ethnic Malay.

**Trang** Lying west of Phattalung and facing the Andaman Sea coastline, Trang is geographically an extension of Krabi, featuring a coast of beaches and islands, and an interior of limestone hills and lush vegetation. Historically, however, Trang was important as a communication link on the old trade route to Nakhon Si Thammarat. Modern economic activity revolves around rubber, oil palms and fishing.

**Southernmost Provinces** Thailand's four southernmost provinces — Satun on the west of the peninsula, Pattani, Yala and Narathiwat — are noticeably influenced by their proximity to neighbouring Malaysia. The population is more Muslim than Buddhist, and mosques rather than temples are the cultural sights — Pattani Central Mosque being the largest in Thailand. Geographically, the Gulf of Thailand shores of Pattani and Narathiwat feature some splendid beaches that are completely undeveloped, while landlocked Yala is characterized by a landscape of mainly mountains and forests, although rubber production makes it the most prosperous and fastest developing province in the far south. Satun, small and remote, facing the Andaman Sea, boasts two major wildlife reserves, Tarutao Marine National Park and Thale Ban National Park. The former, located 31 kilometres (19 miles) off the coast and clustered around 51 islands, combines magnificent scenery with a wealth of marine life, including a wide variety of corals. The 102 square kilometres (39 square miles) of Thale Ban National Park encompass the extraordinary richness of southern rainforests that once covered the peninsula.

# HIGHLANDS AND HILLTRIBES

## NORTHERN THAILAND

Northern Thailand stands apart from other regions of the country as an area of forested highlands traversed by parallel river valleys. The region boasts the country's highest peak, Doi Inthanon, while other upland ranges, although all well below the tree-line, present a picturesquely rugged landscape, parts of which are still comparatively remote. This

is also teak country where work elephants once played an important role in the extraction of logs, but over-exploitation has led to extensive deforestation resulting in the introduction of a logging ban in 1989, legislation that unfortunately came too late to save the finest teak reserves.

It is not only geography that distinguishes the North; history, cultural traditions and ethnic make-up all contribute to a distinct identity. From the late 13th century until the early 1900s the region was largely independent, in its early heyday a thriving kingdom known as Lanna, 'the land of a million rice fields'. Autonomous development, coupled with strong influences from neighbouring Laos and, most especially, Burma (now Myanmar), resulted in distinctive northern arts and architecture. Notably, the temples of Chiang Mai, formerly the capital of Lanna and today Thailand's unofficial second city, are not only far older than those of Bangkok, they are also different in style and decorative detail. Northern handicrafts, too, have remained a thriving tradition, and skills in woodcarving, silverware, celadon pottery and

lacquerware continue to flourish.

Proud of their own heritage, Northerners tend to remain more faithful to long-held values than their Bangkok counterparts and are generally home-loving, thrifty and wary of spending money ostentatiously. The custom of entering the monkhood is still widespread among boys and young men, and ordination ceremonies are particularly elaborate. Festivals in the North are celebrated with greater panache and exuberance than elsewhere in the country, and the local cuisine, with a strong Burmese influence, is a notable treat even in a land renowned for its culinary arts.

The region is strongly coloured by ethnic minorities, hilltribes who continue to pursue independent lifestyles outside mainstream society. Inevitably, the modern world is now beginning to encroach upon tribal ways, yet hilltribe villages with their typically costumed inhabitants continue to characterize much of the northern landscape.

Along with the rest of the country, the North is today changing under the influence of Thailand's recent economic boom years. Chiang Mai, the region's largest city and focal point, is no longer the quaint backwater it once was. Less altered, however, are historic towns such as Chiang Rai, Chiang Saen and Nan, while sleepy highland settlements like Mae Hong Son retain a character all their own, hidden in valleys surrounded by timeless hills.

The focal point of the North is Chiang Mai. It is popularly regarded as the capital of the region, a status arising out of the city's original role as the power centre of the ancient Lanna kingdom which for centuries held sway over most of what is now northern Thailand. Not until early in the present century did Chiang Mai become fully under the control of the central government. Although modern development today extends well beyond the old city walls and the banks of the Ping river (below left), Chiang Mai remains steeped in history. King Mengrai, who founded the city in the late 13th century, remains much revered and is honoured in statues and festival parades, often depicted with his two famous allies, the kings of Sukhothai and Phayao (left). With a largely separate historical development the North has evolved its own art and architectural styles, and venerable temples such as Wat Phra Singh (below) are distinct from those found further south. Not only temple forms, but also decorative motifs, especially woodcarving, along with mural paintings and sculpture, all display characteristics which are unique to the region.

PREVIOUS PAGES
Page 50: Travel in northern Thailand presents stunning vistas of high, forested hills and lush, fertile valleys. Tucked away in this idyllic landscape are rural villages such as Pong Yeang, where the way of life has altered little over the centuries.
Page 51: Traditionally costumed Hmong (Meo) hilltribe people, and other tribal minorities who inhabit the highlands, add a dash of exotic colour to the landscape.

Compared to other parts of the North, Nan is the least visited. Tucked away in the valley of the river of the same name, it lies off the beaten track and the only time it draws attention to itself is during its annual boat racing festival (above). Held in October to mark the end of the annual rains, the regatta is a thrilling affair with teams of oarsmen from all over the province gathering to vie for the honours. But Nan is also a historic town and Wat Chang Kham Vora Viharn (left) and a number of other venerable temples rank among the North's most intriguing monuments.

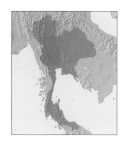

# THE HEART OF THE KINGDOM

## THE CENTRAL PLAINS AND THE WEST

Thailand's Central Plains form the heart of the Kingdom both physically and historically. It was in these fertile, well watered lands that the Thai people became united as a nation, and where life was amply sustained by agricultural abundance. Stretching from the northern hills to the Gulf of Thailand in the south, the plains are dominated by the Chao Phraya, the country's major river formed by the confluence of several streams flowing out of the North. In the course of their historical development the Thais expanded the natural waterways with a network of canals which served as both irrigation channels and communication links for what has traditionally been a waterborne society.

The flat, largely featureless landscape has thus been transformed into the archetypal image of Thailand, a patchwork of paddy fields producing the bulk of the country's all-important rice crop. Scattered throughout the rural scene are villages as well as several sizeable towns, making the region the most densely populated in spite of its agricultural base.

The fertility of the land and the ease of communication afforded by the Chao Phraya river system made the Central Plains a natural site of settlement, and the region encompasses virtually all the important monuments that signpost the evolution of Thai civilization. On the northern edge stand the ruins of Sukhothai, the nation's first capital founded in the 13th century, and its contemporary satellite cities of Si Satchanalai, Phitsanulok and Kamphaeng Phet. These ancient centres form the cradle of Thai civilization, and the art and architecture evolved here constitute the first flowering of indigenous cultural forms, along with religious, social and political systems which set the pattern of nationhood.

To the west of Sukhothai lies Tak, the gateway city to the North and, beyond, Mae Sot on the Burmese border. South is Nakhon Sawan, a populous centre on the north-south trade route, while below is the focal point of Thailand's most formative historical development. Here is the site of Ayutthaya, the capital from 1350 until its destruction at the hands of the Burmese in 1767, and Lopburi, the second capital during Ayutthaya's 17th-century golden era. Both towns are today somewhat shabby provincial centres, although the ruins within their boundaries have been preserved as well as possible to offer an intriguing window on to the past.

The western edge of the Central Plains remains comparatively untouched. The flat lands give way to hills, the tail end of the northern highlands, and the countryside presents a picture of untamed jungle and prime forest cover. This is the location of Huai Kha Khaeng Wildlife Sanctuary, one of the largest and most important nature reserves in the country, where fast dwindling wildlife can still find refuge in Thailand's otherwise increasingly urbanized environment.

The Central Plains form the heart of Thailand, not only in geographical terms but also historically. It was here, on the northern edge of these fertile lowlands, that the nation first came into existence as a sovereign state in the 13th century at Sukhothai, the original capital of the newly united Thais. The chedis and other temple ruins of this once glorious city are today preserved at Sukhothai Historical Park (opposite), Thailand's premier historical site. Dominating the site is Wat Mahathat (above left), noted for its lotus-bud chedi, an architectural style unique to the period, and its decorative detail (above right). To the north is Si Satchanalai, a satellite city, whose ruins are smaller although arguably more evocative than those of Sukhothai, notably the superb Wat Chang Lom (right).

PREVIOUS PAGES
Page 74: Saffron-robed monks ascend the steps to Phra Buddhabat at Saraburi, an important pilgrimage site enshrining a revered Buddha footprint. Page 75: At Lopburi young boys learn the martial art of kick boxing, now a popular sport but originally a form of unarmed combat taught to Thai soldiers during Lopburi's heyday in the Ayutthaya period.

*Straddling the Nan river, south-east of Sukhothai, Phitsanulok is typical of the larger towns in the upper part of the Central Plains. Drawing definition from the river, once an important communication highway, and welcoming the traveller with floating riverside restaurants (above left) and a handful of provincial hotels, the town is today a regional service centre which none the less recalls a more illustrious past. Phitsanulok rose to prominence in the late 14th and early 15th centuries, when it was a strategic point between waning Sukhothai and the rising power of Ayutthaya to the south. Dominating the town is the prang of Wat Phra Si Ratana Mahathat (above right), which dates back to the 14th century and enshrines the important late Sukhothai-style image of Phra Buddha Chinnarat (opposite).*

*The landscape of Thung Salaeng Luang National Park (left) also typifies the area, with the hills of the North meeting the grassy valleys at the beginning of the plains, a habitat for elephants, tigers, boar and deer, as well as nearly 200 bird species.*

West of the Central Plains, the land rises in the area towards the Myanmar border and the scene shifts from the cultivated neatness of the paddy fields to a wilder, more rugged natural beauty. Here, at Thung Yai and Huai Kha Khaeng Wildlife Sanctuaries (above left) *and in the area around Umphang are to be found the best tracts of tropical broadleaf forest still surviving in the country. These sanctuaries shelter a large number of plant and animal species that have vanished elsewhere.*

As in other parts of the world, Thailand's wildlife has suffered from massive deforestation, and yet there remains an exotic variety of flora and fauna. Dendrobium cariniferum (top) *is but one of more than 1,000 species of orchids, while an extraordinary natural diversity is nowhere more apparent than in the insect life, among which there are an estimated 10,000 species of beetles and some 1,200 butterflies* (above right). *Thailand is also particularly rich in bird life, with well over 900 species, including the Wreathed Hornbill* (left), *which is just one of 12 species of hornbill found in the country.*

*With densely forested hills, rivers and waterfalls, the natural scenery around Umphang (above) ranks as arguably the most stunningly beautiful in the whole of the country. In spite of the loss of primary forest cover, Thailand still offers enormous scope for appreciating the bounty of nature. Over 10 per cent of the world's known animals are found here, including at least 280 mammal species, among which is the Tiger (right), Asia's largest species of wild cat. Now endangered animals, tigers are wary and shy, and not easily seen, although it is likely that the protected forests of Huai Kha Khaeng may shelter more of them than anywhere else in Thailand, due to plentiful sources of water, abundant prey and a higher level of conservation.*

Towards the lower end of the Central Plains, in the regions alongside the Chao Phraya river, the sights and scenes become more varied as reminders both of the country's long history and its defining cultural patterns blend in a kaleidoscope of images. The most fascinating town before one reaches the all-important former capital of Ayutthaya is Lopburi. Today a rather uninspiring provincial centre, Lopburi experienced its golden era in the 17th century when King Narai made the town his second capital. The ruins of his palace, approached through massive gateways (left), conjure a good impression of former magnificence.

South of Lopburi, the important Holy Footprint shrine of Phra Buddhabat at Saraburi presents emotive cameos of Buddhist devotion, especially during major festive days such as Khao Pansa (opposite, top left) and in details such as touching the temple bells to make merit (opposite, top right). Elsewhere, the scenes range from the ubiquitous kerbside food stalls (above), so typical of the Thai urban landscape, to the startling fairy-tale-like architecture of Bang Pa-in. A royal summer palace, Bang Pa-in is extraordinary in its eclectic mix of buildings. A Chinese pagoda (opposite, below left) and a superb Thai-style pavilion (opposite, below right) are contrasted by other structures with a European look, which reflect a widespread Thai fascination with Western styles at the turn of the 20th century.

# GATEWAY TO THE NATION

## BANGKOK AND THE SURROUNDING AREA

Thailand's capital, the first sight of the country for most visitors, scarcely matches any preconceived ideas of a fabled city of the Orient, the 'Venice of the East' as it was once known. A few canals do survive, but today's Bangkok appears as a huge concrete sprawl of paved streets bristling with high-rises and clogged with some of the worst traffic congestion in the world. However, beneath the modern and ostensibly western veneer lie captivating sights of temples, palaces, markets and other typically Thai scenes in which the old manages to coexist with the new.

Founded as the capital in 1782, Bangkok is a relatively young city. It has also borne the brunt of Thailand's economic growth and so displays more of the stresses and strains of rapid development than other parts of the country. Beyond the sprawl of the metropolitan area the landscape quickly reverts to a more traditional picture in which a sense of history and natural splendour combine to present images of classic Thailand.

A short distance to the west is Nakhon Pathom, one of the country's oldest settlements and site of what was a Mon capital during the Dvaravati period (6th–11th centuries) and the earliest known centre of Buddhist learning in Thailand. The present town is dominated by the Phra Pathom Chedi, the world's tallest Buddhist monument, which marks the location of an ancient *chedi* that was destroyed in the 11th century.

Further west, modern history is vividly recalled at Kanchanaburi where the infamous Bridge over the River Kwai was constructed by allied POWs of the Japanese during World War II. It is an evocative spot, the memory of those who died working on the bridge surviving in two immaculately kept war cemeteries and a museum. Contrasting with tragic history is the natural beauty of Kanchanaburi province, an area in which jungle-clad hills, wooded river valleys, caves and waterfalls offer some of the most picturesque scenery to be found anywhere in the country.

Different yet equally traditional scenes lie immediately south of Bangkok, with small fishing towns interspersed with shrimp farms strung out along the coast of the Gulf of Thailand. Places of note include Ratchaburi, famed for water jars and other ceramic products, while among tourist sights are a huge crocodile farm and the Ancient City where many of the country's most famous historic buildings have been reconstructed in authentic scale models.

East of the capital leads towards the Khorat Plateau and the vast semi-arid region of I-san. Before this poor rural district is reached is Khao Yai, Thailand's oldest established national park and one of the richest in flora and fauna. The park is remarkable equally for its stunning natural beauty and its wildlife population which includes elephants, tigers, leopards, bears and various species of deer.

Bangkok is today a huge, sprawling modern metropolis lacking any easily discerned downtown area, but the original core of the old royal city still marks a symbolic centre. Located on the east bank of the Chao Phraya, at a spot where the river makes a broad curve, the area is known as Ratanakosin Island and was indeed originally an island when concentric canals linking with the river formed a ring of outer defences. Here are located all the major historical buildings dating from the founding of the city in 1782 and incorporating the regal prestige and capital status recreated after the loss of Ayutthaya. Most famous of all are the Grand Palace (above left) and Wat Phra Keo, Temple of the Emerald Buddha (left and opposite). Both date from the founding of Bangkok as the capital, although the collection of regal apartments that form the Grand Palace was added to by successive monarchs. No longer the official residence of the King, the Palace continues to be used for state functions, and Wat Phra Keo remains the royal chapel. Enshrined in the temple is the statue of the Emerald Buddha (above right), the nation's most sacred image. The statue has three bejewelled costumes, one for each season, which are changed at the appropriate time by the King.

PREVIOUS PAGES
Page 92: The Chao Phraya river was originally Bangkok's main artery. Long since expanding away from the river, the modern city has in recent years returned attention to this historic heart which now bristles with concrete and glass high-rises. Page 93: In classical dance performances and in countless other cultural manifestations Bangkok manages to preserve the old along with the new.

*Temples such as Wat Benchamabophit, the Marble Temple, (below left) are naturally the main focus of religious observance, but not exclusively so. Numerous shrines scattered around the city, such as the memorial to the younger brother of King Rama I at Wat Chana Songkhram (below right), attract devotees who present offerings of flowers, candles and incense. Buddhism is primarily concerned with man's ultimate release from suffering and does not specifically address mundane concerns. At the same time, the popular practice of Buddhism in Thailand incorporates older beliefs based in Brahmanism and animism. Accordingly, various shrines have become widely accepted as having the power to bestow good fortune or grant wishes. The most famous of these in Bangkok is the Erawan Shrine (right), which honours the Hindu god Brahma. Dating from the 1950s, the shrine was originally erected on the advice of Brahman priests to end a spate of misfortune that had plagued the construction of the now demolished Erawan Hotel. It had the desired effect and ever since the shrine has been viewed as an exceptionally potent source of good luck.*

Modern prosperity has not diminished Bangkok's enthusiasm for celebrating traditional festive occasions. As in the past, it is the river which provides a city focal point, and today's deluxe hotels along the banks of the Chao Phraya recreate classic riverine settings for banquets and gala events. Open-air terraces are perfect for celebrating Loy Krathong (above left), with pools reflecting the delicate beauty of krathongs (left) and spectacular firework displays lighting up the sky (above).

*Once known as the 'Venice of the East', Bangkok was essentially a city of waterways, and it was not until the mid 19th century that the first paved roads for wheeled traffic were constructed. Today, the motor car has taken over with a vengeance and most of the original canals have been filled in. Yet sufficient remains for the old pattern to be still visible. The Chao Phraya river continues to carry considerable traffic, whether fast longtail boats (opposite) or slow barges (below right) bringing bulk cargo down from the provinces. Many Bangkokians commute to work via water taxis that ply regular routes up and down the river, while tour boats (right) provide an easy way of taking in the riverside sights.*

*The canals – klongs as they are known in Thai – which were once the main streets, have mostly disappeared from Bangkok proper, but typical scenes of klong life (above) can be seen in Thonburi on the west bank of the river. Here, wooden houses face the water and the usual way of getting about is by boat. Even the shops are aquatic, with fruit, vegetable and grocery sellers peddling their goods from sampans.*

Bangkok is a city of luxuries as much as it is a place of exotic sights, and it offers every opportunity for enjoying the finer things in life. Many of the capital's top hotels rank among the best in the world, with a degree of luxury and, more importantly, a level of service that are unmatched. Every city has its landmark hotel and in Bangkok it is the riverside Oriental. Fully modernized and expanded in recent decades, it dates back to the 19th century and the 'Author's Lounge' of its original wing (above) recalls the charm of a more leisured era of travel. Novelist Joseph Conrad is reputed to have dined here, thereby setting a tradition which the hotel has pursued, naming its suites after other famous literary guests from Somerset Maugham to Graham Greene and Gore Vidal. The hotel also regularly hosts visiting royalty, business tycoons and Hollywood stars.

Catering for those able to indulge expensive tastes are Bangkok's speciality antiques shops (left). Scores of establishments are scattered around the city, while one entire floor of a top shopping plaza is devoted to collector-quality antiques with prices to match.

*A sybaritic city, Bangkok tempts the senses in every way, with the spicy delights of Thai cuisine* (right), *the gorgeous texture of Thai silks* (below left), *and a lively conglomeration of night-clubs and discos* (below right). *Some of the biggest changes the city has undergone in recent years have been in its entertainment offerings. Home-grown attractions, such as Thai kick boxing matches, classical Thai dance shows and, of course, the city's notorious go-go bars, are no longer the only night-time options. Concerts by top-name artistes, performances by visiting ballet companies and orchestras of world renown, and London theatre productions are also now periodic if not daily attractions. Shopping opportunities, too, have developed dramatically and, increasingly, international designer and well-known brand names fill store windows.*

*Excursions beyond Bangkok present a host of things to do and see. Just a short drive away on the city outskirts, the Rose Garden cultural centre and park offers the chance to take a ride on an elephant (left), or watch youngsters put on a display of Thai dances (below left). Alternatively, some 30 kilometres (18 miles) south of the city, there is the world's largest crocodile farm to visit at Samut Prakan, and also worth seeing nearby are replicas of Thailand's most famous monuments at the Ancient City.*

*A day trip south-west of Bangkok, taking an early-morning canal boat, brings one to the famous 'Floating Market' at Damnoen Saduak, where boat-shops selling all manner of produce throng the narrow waterways (opposite) and snacks can be bought from the sampans (below right).*

Travelling west of Bangkok leads to Kanchanaburi, where two rivers, the Kwai Yai and Kwai Noi, flow through idyllic wooded valleys dotted with caves, waterfalls and scenic spots. Beyond, forested hills rise to a saw-tooth mountain range which forms the border with Myanmar and produces a seemingly isolated landscape of a wild and rugged grandeur. This is a historic area, long ago an invasion route for Burmese armies and, in more recent times, the location of the Death Railway and Bridge over the River Kwai (above), built by Allied POWs of the Japanese during World War II.

Besides the bridge at Kanchanaburi, poignant reminders of this dark period in history are found in more than 8,000 graves in two war cemeteries (left).

# TOWARDS THE MIGHTY MEKONG

## NORTH-EASTERN THAILAND

Bordered to the north and east by the Mekong river and Laos, and to the south by Cambodia, the North-east is the largest of Thailand's main topographical regions covering about one-third of the country's land mass. The area comprises a semi-arid plateau with forested mountains in the north-west, where national parks such as Phu Luang and Phu Kradung contain the last remnants of what was once lush forest cover. Otherwise the North-east is intensely rural with a scattering of large towns – Khon Kaen, Ubon Ratchathani, Nakhon Ratchasima (Khorat) and Udon Thani – serving as commercial centres.

Known in Thai as I-san, the North-east is the least changed part of Thailand. The people speak their own melodious dialect, have their own distinctively spiced cuisine, and retain a characteristic hospitable and fun-loving nature. The economy is based almost entirely on agriculture and the majority of north-easterners follow agrarian lifestyles rooted in tradition and dictated by the annual seasonal cycle.

Local culture – music, folk dances, festivals and legends – is better preserved in the North-east than anywhere else in Thailand. Rural traditions are manifest in numerous annual festivals, colourful and often boisterous affairs which punctuate an otherwise arduous agricultural cycle. Among the most spectacular events is the *Bang Fai* (Rocket) Festival, held in the provincial capital of Yasothon, during which giant home-made rockets are fired into the air as an entreaty to the sky god for rains.

I-san is also significant as the location of several sites attesting to the early history of what is now Thailand. Archaeological discoveries at Ban Chiang in the 1970s produced evidence of a Bronze Age civilization that flourished over 5,000 years ago. This predates sites in China and Mesopotamia as the earliest known evidence of an agrarian, bronze-making culture. Elsewhere, prehistoric rock paintings can be seen on the cliffs at Pha Taem in Ubon Ratchathani province.

Moving into the era of recorded history, the North-east possesses the finest examples of ancient Khmer temples to be seen outside Cambodia. Best known of the ruins are the 12th-century temple complexes of Phimai and Prasat Phanom Rung. The architecture of the latter is considerably enhanced by a dominant hill-top location commanding panoramic views of the surrounding countryside.

Historical, topographic and cultural interest are combined in the towns that border the Mekong river, from Nong Khai in the north down to Mukdahan. The most noteworthy monument is Phra That Phanom, the North-east's most sacred shrine located in the small town of the same name, while virtually all the Mekong towns have temples of historic and architectural interest.

What is now north-eastern Thailand was once an outpost of the ancient Khmer empire centred on Angkor in present-day Cambodia. Prasat Phanom Rung (left), with a monumental stairway leading to its impressive hill-top location, is just one of several ruined Khmer temples scattered throughout the region and attesting to the area's distinctive pre-Thai past.

PREVIOUS PAGES
Page 116: *Buddha image near Ubon Ratchathani.*
Page 117: *Old-style bamboo wares for sale at That Phanom.*

Most of the North-east's Khmer temples date from the 12th century and exemplify the architectural genius of ancient Angkor, albeit on a much smaller scale. Many of the larger monuments, such as Prasat Hin Phimai (right), have been restored in recent years, although not all the work has been of even quality. Before it was restored, Muang Tam temple (above) presented an evocative picture of crumbling stonework and overgrown ruins. Fine examples of richly carved lintels and friezes can be seen at both Prasat Hin Phimai and Muang Tam.

The North-east, or I-san as it is known in Thai, occupies a semi-arid and largely deforested plateau where agricultural production from the poor soil scarcely rises above subsistence level. In this least developed region of the country, rural life is sustained mostly without the aid of modern advantages. Seasonal droughts are to be expected, and while the village pump (above right) provides a shower for youngsters, the large earthen jars seen in the background show a prudent provision for water storage. Along with the staple of rice, the North-east also produces a few cash crops, including tomatoes and other vegetables (above left) and tobacco, a common sight laid out in the sun to dry (right). Fish in rivers, streams and lakes provide the main source of protein in the north-eastern diet, and fishermen have devised numerous ways of catching them, not only with nets in various shapes (left), but also with ingeniously designed bamboo traps.

A creaking bullock cart (left) wending its way to and from the fields is an enduring image of I-san's traditional agrarian lifestyle.

*While all Thais love festivals, the north-easterners have their own ways of celebrating not only national events but also numerous other festive occasions that are special to the region or even to a specific town. The people of Sakon Nakhon, for example, celebrate the end of the Buddhist Rains Retreat, Ok Phansa, with boat races (above left) and with the unique custom of fashioning miniature Buddhist temples and shrines out of beeswax (left) to 'make merit'. In different fashion, the beginning of the Rains Retreat, Khao Phansa, is marked in Ubon Ratchathani by the creation of huge and beautifully carved wax candles which are paraded through the town before being presented to local temples (above).*

*The liveliest event in the north-eastern calendar, however, is the Rocket Festival, most elaborately celebrated at Yasothon (opposite, below). At this time in May villagers make huge rockets by packing gunpowder into lengths of plastic tubing, some several metres long, which are launched into the air as a reminder to the sky god to send the annual rains. The two-day event is accompanied by parades, fairs and much high-spirited revelry.*

Not all of the eastern seaboard has succumbed to modern development and working fishing boats (above) and other traditional coastal sights are found beyond Pattaya, notably in the neighbouring province of Rayong. Most visited of the resorts on this part of the coast is Koh Samet (right), a small island noted for its sandy beaches, secluded coves and coral reefs. Long popular with budget travellers, Koh Samet is officially designated as a national park and efforts are being made to protect the environment.

*Off the coast of Trat province, which abuts Cambodia, lies Koh Chang, or 'Elephant Island', the most unspoilt of all the resort areas of the eastern seaboard. With accommodation still limited to mostly thatched bungalows* (left) *and simple hotels with sea views* (top), *the island remains close to the tropical paradise of travel brochures. Visitors – few so far – can generally lay claim to nearly a whole palm-fringed beach for themselves* (right), *and even then there are plenty of other spots to escape to. Koh Chang itself is 30 kilometres (18 miles) long and 8 kilometres (5 miles) at its widest point, and it is only one in an archipelago of 52 islands, many of them uninhabited. Offshore, fish traps* (above) *attest to the unchanged lifestyle of the local people.*

# TROPICAL BEACHES AND OFFSHORE ISLANDS

## SOUTHERN THAILAND

Forming a long narrow peninsula, southern Thailand stretches some 1,200 kilometres (750 miles) from just below Bangkok to the Malaysian border. The land is characterized by a mountainous spine and humped limestone karst formations which appear both as cliffs and offshore islets, while the coastline is indented with coves and beaches. Numerous islands, including the country's largest, Phuket, dot the coastal waters.

Topographically and, to a large extent, culturally the region divides into two, the upper and lower south. The former, which extends down to Chumphon, faces the Gulf of Thailand to the east and is bordered to the west by Myanmar (Burma). Most of the coastline is now taken over by beach resorts, notably Cha-am and Hua Hin which are within easy driving distance from Bangkok, although the traditional occupation of fishing still provides the main livelihood for the coastal villages. Away from the sea, cultivation on the narrow coastal plain is dominated by plantations, mostly pineapple.

The history of the upper south is linked closely with that of the Central Plains. The main town of the area, Phetchaburi, was an important provincial centre during the Ayutthaya and early Bangkok periods and still boasts several venerable temples, as well as a 19th-century hilltop palace built by King Rama IV. Hua Hin retains regal connections to this day, being the site of a summer palace which is still used by the Royal Family.

Beyond Chumphon, the lower south is distinguished by a more truly tropical climate and the last vestiges of Thailand's rainforests. The border with Myanmar ends near the town of Ranong and the Thai shore faces both the Andaman Sea, on the west, and the Gulf of Thailand to the east. The landscape is defined by rubber and coconut plantations which, along with tin mining in Phuket and fishing on both coasts, have been the traditional activities of the region.

The coastal ports of the lower south were once staging posts on the sea route from India to China, while the area also boasts important sites dating back to the Srivijaya period (8th–13th centuries). But although ancient settlements, such as Nakhon Si Thammarat and Songkhla, retain vestiges of the past, modern commercial development in the South is largely uninspiring, as witnessed in the region's major business hub, Hat Yai. A strong Muslim influence typifies what is a distinctive southern culture.

The lower south is best known today as the nation's top tourist attraction. Phuket island and Krabi, on the Andaman coast, and Samui island in the Gulf can all claim tropical beaches that rank among the best in the world.

*Although best known for its beaches and offshore islands, the long narrow peninsula of southern Thailand displays different characteristics along its considerable length and between its western and eastern shores. The first place of note on a journey south from Bangkok is Phetchaburi. The town has a history dating back to the Khmer period and is fascinating for its several historic temples. Wat Mahathat, instantly identifiable by its striking* prangs *(opposite),* enshrines a number of Buddha images *(left), while two other temples, Wat Yai Suwannaram and Wat Ko Keo Suttharam, have some fine mural paintings. Beyond Phetchaburi, beach resorts in the upper south begin with Cha-am, a small unpretentious town with seafront shops* (below left) *facing a sandy beach* (below).

PREVIOUS PAGES
Page 142: *The white beaches and lush tropical hinterland of Koh Samui are typical of the island and the coastal scenery of the far south.* Page 143: *Classical Manhora dancers are part of the southern region's unique cultural tradition.*

*At Chumphon, roughly half-way down the peninsula's Gulf coast, the climate and scenery start to become more tropical. This is the beginning of Thailand's deep south, where roadside fruit stalls (left) and Pig-tailed Macaques trained to collect coconuts (above left) are ubiquitous images.*

*Offshore islands, such as Koh Tao, with pristine beaches (opposite, below), are more numerous along the far southern coast, and many of them are now provided with basic beach bungalows (above) that are popular with independent travellers. Surat Thani, a key town on the Gulf coast, serves as the ferry port for many of the outlying islands. During its Chak Phra festival at the end of the Buddhist Rains Retreat, revered Buddha images are transported in processions on decorated boats (opposite, above) and elaborate carriages.*

The Koh Samui/Ang Thong archipelago in the Gulf of Thailand comprises some 80 tropical islands. The 50 limestone islands of Ang Thong (above), which can be visited by boat from Koh Samui, were designated a marine national park in 1980. Covered in pristine forest and edged with white sandy beaches, almost all of Ang Thong's islands are uninhabited.

By contrast, nearby Samui island has in recent years become one of Thailand's leading beach destinations. Luckily, the island is large enough to sustain a tourist boom: its fine palm-fringed beaches (above left) and clear waters, ideal for snorkelling and diving (opposite, below), mostly retain an idyllic appearance and modern infrastructure has largely been restricted to developments in keeping with the natural surroundings, as at the Imperial Boat House Hotel (left).

Across the peninsula on the shores of the Andaman Sea lie Satun and Trang, provinces little visited by travellers, although off the coast of Satun is the Tarutao group of islands, the country's first marine national park. To the north is Krabi province where the fabulous scenery of the twin Phi Phi islands presents the archetypal image of a tropical hideaway, with limestone cliffs, palm groves and white sandy beaches. Shaped like a lopsided butterfly, the larger of the two islands, Phi Phi Don (above), is formed by a narrow strand joining two 'wings' of which the left has high shrub-covered hills and the right a jungle-clad spine flanked on either side by palm-fringed beaches. Most boats to the islands arrive at Tonsai Bay (left), to the right of the isthmus; the village here has expanded to provide more facilities for visitors, especially divers.

Neighbouring Phi Phi Le island has more dramatic scenery than Phi Phi Don and is uninhabited. Though there is only one hotel on Phi Phi Don, many of its bays support beach bungalow resorts so tourism has left its mark on what was once, like its sister island, a site of untouched natural beauty. None the less, pristine beaches are still to be found (above) and the waters surrounding both islands abound in colourful corals and reef life. With spirit shrines (right) adding an exotic touch to what is still superb scenery, Phi Phi remains captivating, and its status as part of the Had Nopparat Marine National Park should afford it protection from excess development.

The coastlines of both Krabi (left) and neighbouring Phang-Nga province are among the most scenic in the entire South. Besides picturesque fishing boats (below left) and the stilted villages of fishing communities (below), the coastal scenery is characterized by karst limestone formations thrown up by shifts in the earth's crust some 75 million years ago. On land this has formed sheer cliffs while out at sea the phenomenon appears as hauntingly sculpted islands and rocky outcrops.

The most startling example of this region's seascape is Phang-Nga Bay, where hundreds of karst outcrops dot the water. Fantastically shaped by erosion over the millennia and swathed in tangles of creepers and shrubs, some of the outcrops rise sheer, others are humped or jagged. Some are little more than rocks, while others have precipitous cliffs large enough to conceal caves and grottoes. Most famous of all is the so-called James Bond island (opposite) which was featured in the 1970s film The Man with the Golden Gun.

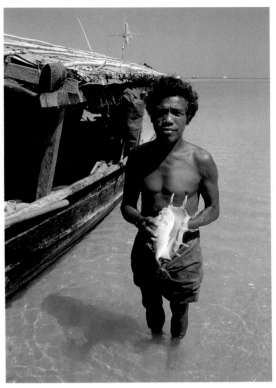

*To the north of Phuket lie the Marine National Parks of the beautiful Similan Islands and, beyond, the equally idyllic Surin Islands. Pristine, white-sand coves, crystal-clear turquoise waters, and a profusion of exotic marine life draw visitors to their unspoilt shores. Both areas offer top-class diving and snorkelling and the Similans (left and above), in particular, have a breathtaking variety of exciting sites to dive.*

*Little developed, and with few facilities, both groups of islands are largely uninhabited except for Park officials and, on Koh Surin Tai, a community of traditional island people known as 'sea gypsies' (top).*

# INDEX

## PHOTOGRAPHIC ACKNOWLEDGEMENTS

The publishers extend their thanks to the following people who kindly loaned their photographs for inclusion in this book. With the exception of those listed below, the photographs in the book were taken by **Gerald Cubitt**.

**Artasia Press (John Everingham):** 13 (left), 70 (above), 97 (above), 129 (above), 133, 155 (above)

**Asia Images (Matthew Burns):** 153 (below right), 155 (below); **(Allen W. Hopkins):** 127 (below), 136 (below)

**Axiom (Jim Holmes):** 88 (above)

**Crescent Press Agency (David Henley):** 156 (above)

**Ron Emmons:** 14 (below), 52 (above), 54 (above and below left), 55, 62 (above left), 63 (above right)

**Footprints (Nick Hanna):** 139 (below), 150 (above right); **(Haydn Jones):** 57 (above)

**Michael Freeman:** 94 (above right), 97 (below left and below right), 103 (below right), 164 (centre)

**Jill Gocher:** 1, 2, 3, 28 (left), 43 (above left), 109 (below right), 157 (below left and below right), 158 (above left and below), 161 (above), 163 (below), 164 (top)

**Mark Graham:** 152 (above right)

**David Holdsworth:** 65 (above right and below), 107 (top)

**The Hutchison Library (Michael MacIntyre):** 10

**Christina Jansen:** 153 (above right)

**Maurice Joseph:** 5, 99 (below left)

**Norma Joseph:** 41 (centre left)

**Khun Akorn Restaurant:** 37, 109 (above)

**Neil McAllister:** 99 (below right), 151 (below)

**Keith Mundy:** 22, 25 (above), 34 (right), 35 (above right), 74, 81 (below right), 82 (below left and below right), 88 (below), 89 (above left and above right), 96 (above), 103 (below left), 120 (top left, centre and below), 123 (below left), 128 (above left and below left), 129 (below), 173 (above right)

**New Holland (Publishers) Ltd:** 123 (below right)

**Oceanic Impressions (Mark Strickland):** 19 (above right), 138 (top, middle and below left), 162 (above), 166 (all three subjects), 167, 168 (below left), 171 (above and below), 172, 173 (below right)

**The Oriental Hotel, Bangkok:** 25 (below)

**PhotoBank (Adrian Baker):** 106, 135 (above); **(Jeanetta Baker):** 42 (left); **(Peter Baker):** 11, 32, 39, 83 (above), 110 (above), 113 (above right), 123 (above), 134 (above), 144 (below right), 146 (below left), 147 (below), 165, 170 (above right)

**PictureBank Photo Library:** 53 (above), 99 (above), 113 (below), 122 (above), 143, 169 (above and below)

**Tourism Authority of Thailand:** 20, 31, 35 (above left), 41 (above right and below left), 96 (below), 109 (below left), 122 (below right), 131 (below left), 151 (above), 157 (above right), 170 (below)

**Travel Ink (Abbie Enock):** 29, 65 (above left), 66 (above); **(Allan Hartley):** 75, 91 (above)

**Zefa Pictures:** 154 (left)